D1493252

FIELD GUIDE *to*
HENDRICK'S
⟨ GIN ⟩

VOLUME TWO

TABLE *of* CONTENTS

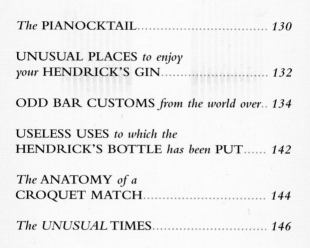

A second edition of the original Field Guide to Hendrick's Gin first published in Great Britain in 2005, and fussed over since then while profligately sipping many of the new concoctions that have been collected since and described herein.

The Field Guide to Hendrick's Gin Volume II is published privately by William Grant & Sons Ltd. Yet we assure you, it can be read respectably in public.

This book is available from William Grant & Sons Ltd. or by visiting Hendricksgin.com

All rights reserved. No part of this publication may be reproduced in any form or by any means without prior permission of the copyright holder.

© 2009 WILLIAM GRANT & SONS LTD. SIP RESPONSIBLY.

HENDRICK'S GIN
It's not for everyone.

*I*f you were to survey any given group of individuals about our gin, you would find that a rather small minority fiercely adores Hendrick's. However, if the truth be told, a vast majority of people has not an inkling that such a wonderfully peculiar gin even exists.

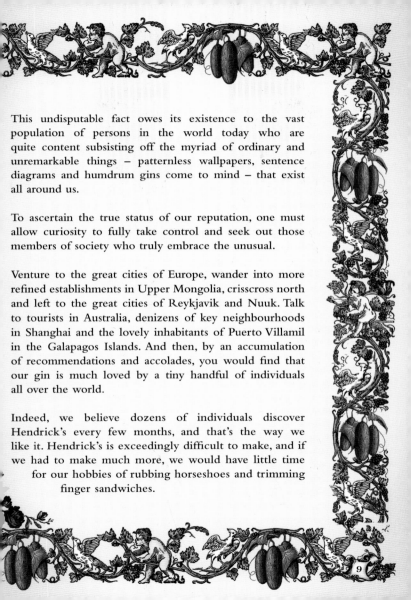

This undisputable fact owes its existence to the vast population of persons in the world today who are quite content subsisting off the myriad of ordinary and unremarkable things – patternless wallpapers, sentence diagrams and humdrum gins come to mind – that exist all around us.

To ascertain the true status of our reputation, one must allow curiosity to fully take control and seek out those members of society who truly embrace the unusual.

Venture to the great cities of Europe, wander into more refined establishments in Upper Mongolia, crisscross north and left to the great cities of Reykjavik and Nuuk. Talk to tourists in Australia, denizens of key neighbourhoods in Shanghai and the lovely inhabitants of Puerto Villamil in the Galapagos Islands. And then, by an accumulation of recommendations and accolades, you would find that our gin is much loved by a tiny handful of individuals all over the world.

Indeed, we believe dozens of individuals discover Hendrick's every few months, and that's the way we like it. Hendrick's is exceedingly difficult to make, and if we had to make much more, we would have little time for our hobbies of rubbing horseshoes and trimming finger sandwiches.

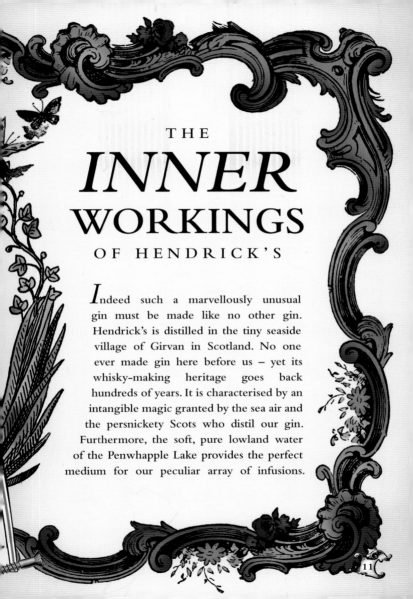

THE
INNER
WORKINGS
OF HENDRICK'S

*I*ndeed such a marvellously unusual gin must be made like no other gin. Hendrick's is distilled in the tiny seaside village of Girvan in Scotland. No one ever made gin here before us – yet its whisky-making heritage goes back hundreds of years. It is characterised by an intangible magic granted by the sea air and the persnickety Scots who distil our gin. Furthermore, the soft, pure lowland water of the Penwhapple Lake provides the perfect medium for our peculiar array of infusions.

Our APPROACH
to PRODUCTION *is*
SMALL-MINDED
(TO SAY THE LEAST!)

*T*ypically, "small batch" refers to one thousand litres. For us, that would be a crudely large quantity. We prefer to handcraft Hendrick's in miniscule batches of 450 litres at a time. The smaller the batch, the more overparticular our stillman can be. Said stillman, Alan Rimmer is so fussy about his gin – a fact exhibited by his exhaustive notebooks detailing the botanical quotients of every batch of Hendrick's – he permits no one else to manage the distillation.

MEET OUR

DELECTABLY ODD BOTANICALS

The peculiar unusualness of Hendrick's resides in our subtle and sensually wondrous botanical signature of flowers, roots, fruits and seeds from the world over.

fig. 1
Cubeb Berries

fig. 2
Chamomile

fig. 11
Lemon Peel

fig. 10
Angelica Root

fig. 9
Orris Root

HENDRICK
DISTILLED and BOTTLED IN SCOTL
GIN
EST. 1886

14

fig. 3
Caraway Seeds

fig. 5
Meadowsweet

fig. 6
Orange Peel

fig. 4
Elderflower

fig. 8
Coriander

fig. 7
Juniper

AND NOW FOR THE
MOST CURIOUS PART...

Our eleven botanicals are analogous to a spectacular chorus of flavours. They function to complement and set the stage for our delicious duet of infusions: rose petal and cucumber. Together, these two odd bedfellows represent the finishing touch that makes our oddness so sublime.

A TALE OF
TWO STILLS

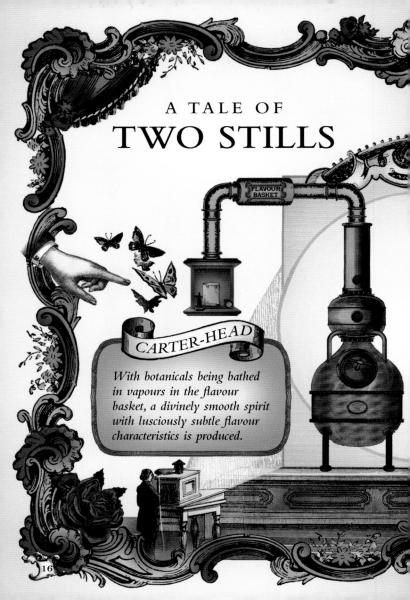

CARTER-HEAD

With botanicals being bathed in vapours in the flavour basket, a divinely smooth spirit with lusciously subtle flavour characteristics is produced.

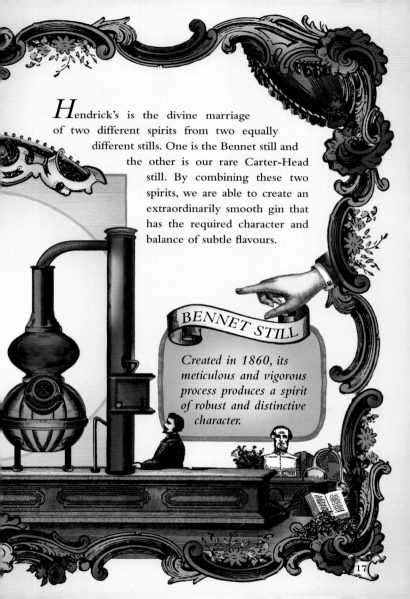

Hendrick's is the divine marriage of two different spirits from two equally different stills. One is the Bennet still and the other is our rare Carter-Head still. By combining these two spirits, we are able to create an extraordinarily smooth gin that has the required character and balance of subtle flavours.

BENNET STILL

Created in 1860, its meticulous and vigorous process produces a spirit of robust and distinctive character.

17

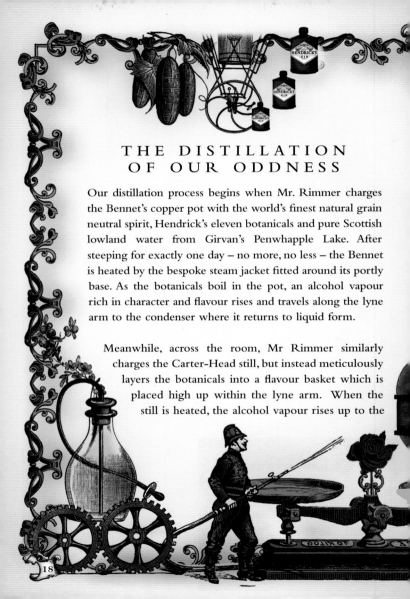

THE DISTILLATION
OF OUR ODDNESS

Our distillation process begins when Mr. Rimmer charges the Bennet's copper pot with the world's finest natural grain neutral spirit, Hendrick's eleven botanicals and pure Scottish lowland water from Girvan's Penwhapple Lake. After steeping for exactly one day – no more, no less – the Bennet is heated by the bespoke steam jacket fitted around its portly base. As the botanicals boil in the pot, an alcohol vapour rich in character and flavour rises and travels along the lyne arm to the condenser where it returns to liquid form.

Meanwhile, across the room, Mr Rimmer similarly charges the Carter-Head still, but instead meticulously layers the botanicals into a flavour basket which is placed high up within the lyne arm. When the still is heated, the alcohol vapour rises up to the flavour basket bathing the botanicals in warm vapour, slowly extracting the flavour which is more subtle and smooth.

From each still's condenser, Mr. Rimmer proceeds to collect only the best bit, called the heart *(or one might say the middle cut)*. He then marries the two spirits in proportions so secret that only those in his tiny inner circle — so tiny it is barely a circle — are privy to the formula.

The COUP
de GRÂCE

*I*mmediately after the intricate and mysterious marrying process adjourns, Hendrick's is infused with *rose* and *cucumber*. We use not just any rose, but the remarkable Bulgarian Rosa Damascena selected for its subtle floral essences, and our cucumbers are specifically selected to represent the epitome of cucumberness. Together the effect is like nothing else in the world. No other gin tastes like Hendrick's as no other gin is made like it.

21

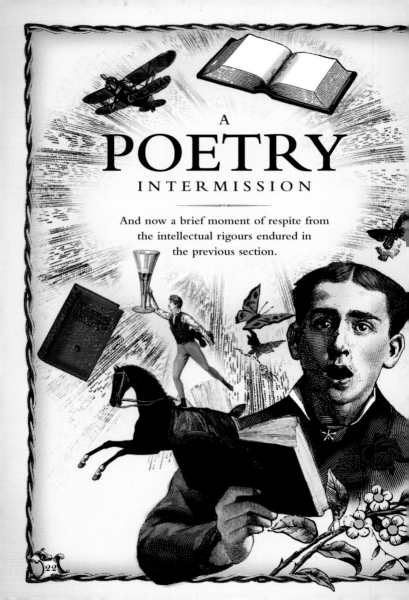

A
POETRY
INTERMISSION

And now a brief moment of respite from
the intellectual rigours endured in
the previous section.

AN ACT OF
UNCOMMON BRAVERY

Like legs and hosiery,
Like camembert with wine
When the world pondered gin
It imprisoned it with lime.

Yet an uncommon few
With heretic flavour on the mind
Have fled convention
Toward something more sublime.

Abandoning all citrus,
They've cast default choices asunder.
With true courage, they garnish
Their Hendrick's with
CUCUMBER.

23

ODE AGAINST THE ORDINARY

The ordinary is common.

The usual is typical.

Everyday is too often.

Down with commodities.

Three cheers for the offbeat!

Bravo to oddities!

Embrace the remarkable.

Be scintillating.

Let your iconoclast sparkle.

Embrace the strange.

Cuddle the ironic.

Consider a cucumber
In your gin and tonic.

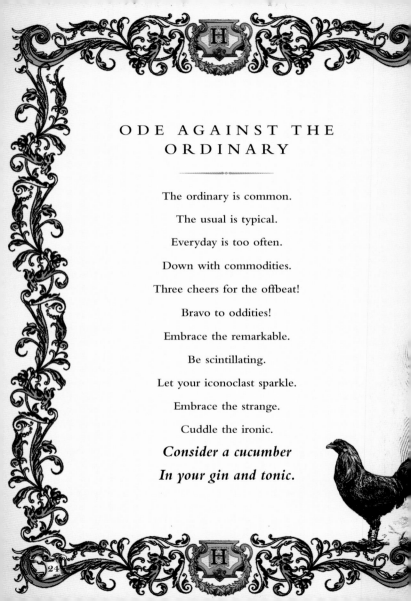

PLEASE EXCUSE
YET ANOTHER POEM

DRINK THE PATH
NOT TAKEN

Step away from normal,
Please, we insist.
Hold off from the humdrum.
Really, resist.

Put down that beer.
Try something eccentric.
For goodness sakes,

Let us pour you a Hendrick's.

27

THE CONNOISSEUR'S
GIN
TASTING
TERMINOLOGY

*T*here is much involved in the enjoyment of a gin as spectacular as Hendrick's. These sensory categories represent serious and weighty considerations that should be put to use. We suggest they be used exclusively in educated company. Representing a curious mixture of Wodehousian upper-class English and Scots...

THE WHIFF

The olfactory experience that occurs when inhaling the aromatic atmosphere surrounding an opened bottle (the neat plop of a cork being freed enhances "the whiff" substantially).

THE
TINKLE

Both of sound and the play of light as gin is poured into a glass. Graceful technique can exalt the tinkle to new heights.

THE
TONGUE-JIG

The giddy feeling of gin dancing within the mouth (no music required!).

THE
KICK

The initial tasting, when the notes of the flavour begin to make themselves heard. Usage example: "I say, old bean, this little number kicks a smidgeon beedy barkit wi' a rather marvellous birl, eh?"

THE
GLINT

An elusive sparkle in the eye of the taster, often accompanied by an almost sinister smile, as he or she comes to a full realisation of the relative majesty of the gin in question, and the quiet anticipation of a continued liaison.

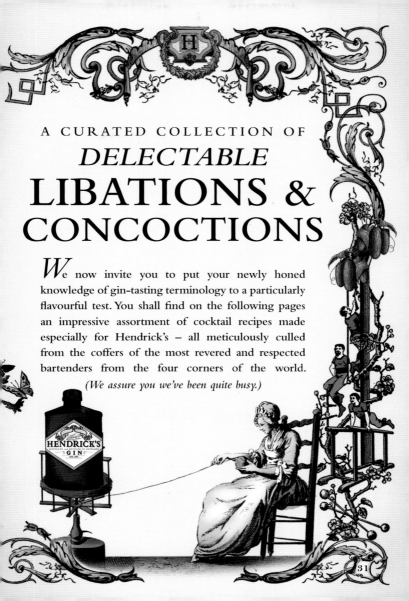

A CURATED COLLECTION OF

DELECTABLE
LIBATIONS &
CONCOCTIONS

*W*e now invite you to put your newly honed knowledge of gin-tasting terminology to a particularly flavourful test. You shall find on the following pages an impressive assortment of cocktail recipes made especially for Hendrick's – all meticulously culled from the coffers of the most revered and respected bartenders from the four corners of the world.

(We assure you we've been quite busy.)

AMBER
ROOM

BARTENDER: Stephan Berg
WORKING PLACE: The Bitter Truth
CITY: Berlin | COUNTRY: Germany

INGREDIENTS

¾ oz (20ml) Hendrick's Gin
¾ oz (20ml) Noilly Prat® Ambré
¼ oz (7ml) elderflower liqueur
2 dashes (The Bitter Truth®) orange bitters

PREPARATION

Stir well with ice and strain into a
cocktail glass. Garnish with a
lemon twist.

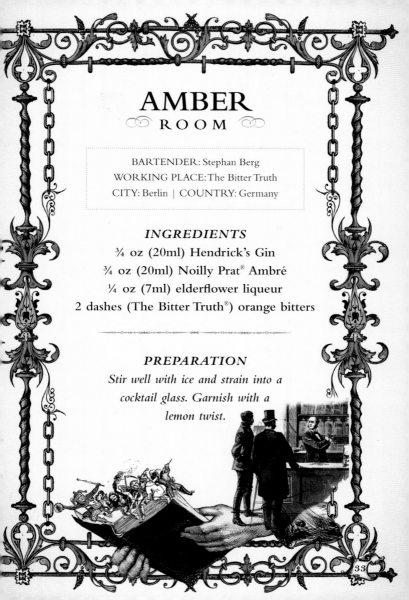

GIMLET

GRENADE

BARTENDER: Jason Chan
WORKING PLACE: Seamstress
CITY: Melbourne | COUNTRY: Australia

INGREDIENTS

1¾ oz (50ml) Hendrick's Gin

¾ oz (20ml) lime juice

¾ oz (20ml) pomegranate syrup

2 slices of cucumber

6-8 mint leaves

1 bar spoon (5ml) sugar syrup 1:1

PREPARATION

Muddle cucumber with the sugar syrup.
Add mint leaves and the remaining
ingredients and shake. Double strain
and serve in a chilled cocktail glass.
Garnish with a mint leaf.

35

EL EXILO
DE LA ROSA

BARTENDER: Paul Bordonaba
WORKING PLACE: El Museo Del Whisky
CITY: San Sebastian | COUNTRY: Spain

INGREDIENTS

1 oz (30ml) Hendrick's Gin
¼ oz (7ml) mango syrup
2 pieces of lime peel
2 pieces of orange peel
dash of blue curaçao spray
tonic water

PREPARATION

*Pour the syrup, the pieces of fruit peel and Hendrick's
Gin into a highball glass. Add a lot of ice. Top up with
tonic water. Garnish with two slices of cucumber
and add the dash of blue curaçao.*

GIN
ROSE LANE

BARTENDER: Roman Milostivy
WORKING PLACE: The Ritz
CITY: Moscow | COUNTRY: Russia

INGREDIENTS

1¾ oz (50ml) Hendrick's Gin
½ oz (15ml) hibiscus (karkade) syrup★
1 oz (30ml) fresh grapefruit juice
1 dash grapefruit bitters

PREPARATION

Shaken and served straight up in a chilled cocktail glass, garnished depending on the occasion (or availability) with a hibiscus petal or simply a grapefruit twist.

★To make hibiscus (karkade) syrup: take 5 teaspoons of hibiscus herbal tea, pour 15 oz (500ml) hot water and let it brew for about 5 minutes. Fine strain and add the same amount of sugar. Stir until dissolved and cool it down.

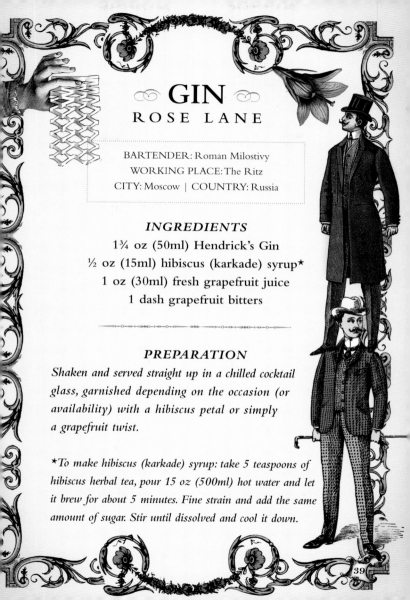

ELDERFLOWER
⊷ GIN FIX ⊷

BARTENDER: Hannah Lanfear
WORKING PLACE: Bungalow 8 at St Martin's Lane
CITY: London | COUNTRY: England

INGREDIENTS
1 oz (25ml) Hendrick's Gin
1 oz (25ml) elderflower liqueur
¾ oz (22.5ml) lemon juice
½ oz (15ml) sugar syrup

PREPARATION
*Build with crushed ice and garnish with
a lemon wedge and a flower.*

HENDRICK'S
GARDEN

BARTENDER: Adelino Figueira
WORKING PLACE: O Cocktail
CITY: Madeira | COUNTRY: Portugal

INGREDIENTS

1½ oz (45ml) Hendrick's Gin
½ oz (15ml) Madeira Wine Verdelho★
½ oz (15ml) Roses™ lime cordial
½ oz (15ml) cranberry or blackberry juice

PREPARATION

*Mix all of the ingredients in a mixing glass
and serve in a cocktail glass. Garnish with a
small cucumber and a white rose petal.*
★ *Verdelho: "medium dry"*

43

LADY
HENDRICK'S

BARTENDER: Mark Ward
WORKING PLACE: Hugo's
CITY: Sydney | COUNTRY: Australia

INGREDIENTS

1¾ oz (50ml) Hendrick's Gin
¼ oz (10ml) Cinzano® Bianco vermouth
¼ oz (10ml) Massenez® Pomme Verte
⅛ oz (5ml) organic elderflower cordial
2 Kaffir lime leaves
zest of 1 lime

PREPARATION

*Snap lime zest into glass to layer the glass with lime oils,
then pour ingredients into a martini pitcher – with 2 torn
Kaffir lime leaves, stir and then strain into glass.
Garnish with a floating Kaffir lime leaf.*

THE
GALLONE

BARTENDER: Giuseppe Gallo
WORKING PLACE: Purple Bar at Sanderson
CITY: London | COUNTRY: England

INGREDIENTS

1¾ oz (50ml) Hendrick's Gin
1 oz (25ml) Martini Bitters or Campari®
1 oz (25ml) Cynar®
1 dash of Cardamom bitters

PREPARATION

Stir all of the ingredients in a mixing glass.
Strain into a martini glass and garnish
with a cucumber slice float.

ORCHARD
COOLER

BARTENDER: Greg Akoka
WORKING PLACE: Bar Aqua
COUNTRY: Singapore

INGREDIENTS

1½ oz (40ml) Hendrick's Gin

¾ oz (20ml) cinnamon

1 oz (30ml) pear purée

½ oz (15ml) lemon juice

1 bar spoon (5ml) simple syrup

1¾ oz (50ml) apple juice

PREPARATION

Shake and strain over cubed ice into a cooler,
or build and stir with crushed ice.
Garnish with a lemon wedge and a pear fan.

THE
WALLFLOWER

BARTENDER: Jackie Patterson
WORKING PLACE: Zinnia
CITY: San Francisco | COUNTRY: USA

INGREDIENTS

1½ oz (40ml) Hendrick's Gin

¾ oz (20ml) Galliano®

¾ oz (20ml) orange juice

½ oz (15ml) lemon juice

½ a bar spoon of rose water

PREPARATION

*Shake ingredients on ice and
strain into a chilled coupe.
Garnish with a nasturtium petal.*

THE PICKLED
PIG

BARTENDER: Eric Alperin
WORKING PLACE: Varnish
CITY: Los Angeles | COUNTRY: USA

INGREDIENTS

2 oz (60ml) Hendrick's Gin
½ oz (15ml) live red wine vinegar infused with bacon
½ oz (15ml) cucumber simple syrup
2 drops of rose water

PREPARATION

*Stir ingredients and serve up in a beautiful
chilled cocktail coupe. Garnish with a dried rose
petal with small pieces of crisply fried bacon.*

TANABATA
∽ MIST ∾

BARTENDER: Kenta Goto
WORKING PLACE: Pegu
CITY: New York City | COUNTRY: USA

INGREDIENTS

2 oz (60ml) Hendrick's Gin
¼ oz (7ml) lemon juice
½ oz (15ml) simple syrup
1 oz (30ml) Calpico®
6 drops absinthe

PREPARATION

*Lightly stir all of the ingredients without ice
in a mixing glass. Pour them into a
rocks glass filled with crushed ice.
Garnish with a spray mist of absinthe
over the glass for aroma.*

THE
⚛ ELLISON ⚛

BARTENDER: Charles Hardwick
WORKING PLACE: Blue Owl
CITY: New York City | COUNTRY: USA

INGREDIENTS

1¾ oz (50ml) Hendrick's Gin
¾ oz (20ml) simple syrup
¾ oz (20ml) fresh lime juice
3 thin cucumber slices
4 to 5 mint leaves
dash Angostura bitters®

PREPARATION

*Lightly muddle the mint and cucumber slices
along with a dash of simple syrup in the glass half
of a Boston shaker. Add lime juice, the rest of
the simple syrup, the Hendrick's and the bitters,
along with ice. Shake vigorously and
strain into a chilled cocktail glass.
Garnish with a thin slice of cucumber
and mint leaves.*

TIPPLING
TEA

BARTENDER: Christian Sanders
WORKING PLACE: Love Hate
CITY: Miami | COUNTRY: USA

INGREDIENTS

2 oz (60ml) Hendrick's Gin

1½ oz (40ml) bergamot & chamomile cordial★

¼ oz (7ml) lemon juice

¼ oz (7ml) lemon grass syrup

½ oz (15ml) cucumber juice

1 bar spoon fresh ginger juice

PREPARATION

In a mixing glass, add all of the ingredients and gently shake. Strain into a champagne coupe and float a cucumber wheel onto the drink, rub the rim with fresh sage and place the leaf onto the cucumber slice, then top the cocktail with a touch of cracked pepper.

★1 part bergamot syrup, 1 part chamomile syrup,
1 part strongly brewed chamomile tea

JAPANESE
∽ BASIL CUP ∽

BARTENDER: Angelo Vieira
WORKING PLACE: The Florida Room at Delano
CITY: Miami | COUNTRY: USA

INGREDIENTS

1½ oz (40ml) Hendrick's Gin
3 basil leaves gently pressed
¾ oz (20ml) elderflower liqueur
1½ oz (40ml) sake
½ oz (15ml) simple syrup
½ oz (15ml) fresh lemon juice
splash soda top

PREPARATION

Shake all ingredients and pour into a 12 oz (330ml)
pewter cup over crushed ice, add a splash of soda.
Garnish with basil leaves.

MR.
PICKLES

BARTENDER: Daniel Hyatt
WORKING PLACE: Alembic
CITY: San Francisco | COUNTRY: USA

INGREDIENTS
2 oz (60ml) Hendrick's Gin
½ oz (15ml) honey
1 bar spoon strong black tea
1 bar spoon apple cider vinegar

PREPARATION
Ice and stir well into a chilled coupe.
Garnish with a thin slice of black radish
and a demitasse spoon with a little
American Sturgeon Caviar.

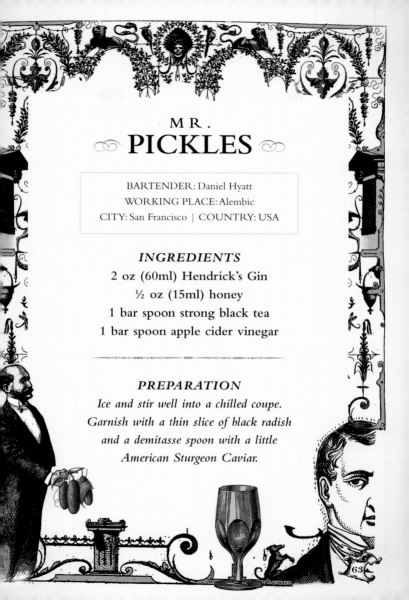

MRS.
TEA

BARTENDER: Kirk Estestopinal
WORKING PLACE: Formerly of Violet Hour in Chicago
CITY: New Orleans | COUNTRY: USA

INGREDIENTS
2 oz (60ml) Hendrick's Gin
(infused with red or jasmine tea★)
¾ oz (20ml) lemon juice
½ oz (15ml) demerara simple syrup
½ oz (15ml) elderflower liqueur

PREPARATION
Combine the ingredients with ice and shake. Strain into a chilled cocktail glass and garnish with an edible flower soaked in orange flower water.

★For the infusion, soak 2 tablespoons loose leaf tea in a bottle of Hendrick's Gin for 1 hour. Tea strain and re-bottle. This is shelf stable.

SUB
ROSA

BARTENDER: Christian Gaal
WORKING PLACE: Apothecary
CITY: Philadelphia | COUNTRY: USA

INGREDIENTS

1½ oz (40ml) Hendrick's Gin

½ oz (15ml) Torani Amer® Picon

½ oz (15ml) simple Fée Brothers Falernum®

¾ oz (20ml) egg white

1 dash of double cream

1 drop rose water

10 drops tincture of Yohimbe

PREPARATION

*In a mixing tin, combine the egg white
and the spring from a Hawthorne strainer.
Shake until it is frothy. Remove spring, and add
all of the remaining ingredients. Shake well, strain
into a small cocktail glass. Garnish with a cucumber
slice and a pinch of grated nutmeg.*

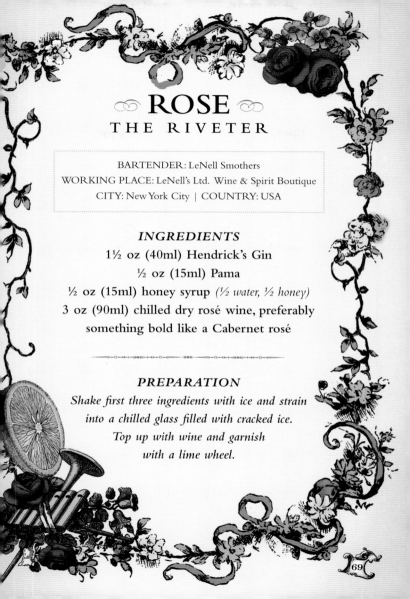

ROSE
THE RIVETER

BARTENDER: LeNell Smothers
WORKING PLACE: LeNell's Ltd. Wine & Spirit Boutique
CITY: New York City | COUNTRY: USA

INGREDIENTS
1½ oz (40ml) Hendrick's Gin
½ oz (15ml) Pama
½ oz (15ml) honey syrup *(½ water, ½ honey)*
3 oz (90ml) chilled dry rosé wine, preferably
something bold like a Cabernet rosé

PREPARATION
*Shake first three ingredients with ice and strain
into a chilled glass filled with cracked ice.
Top up with wine and garnish
with a lime wheel.*

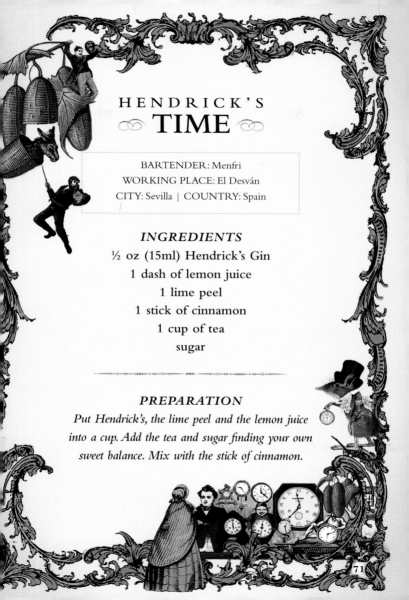

HENDRICK'S
TIME

BARTENDER: Menfri
WORKING PLACE: El Desván
CITY: Sevilla | COUNTRY: Spain

INGREDIENTS
½ oz (15ml) Hendrick's Gin
1 dash of lemon juice
1 lime peel
1 stick of cinnamon
1 cup of tea
sugar

PREPARATION
*Put Hendrick's, the lime peel and the lemon juice
into a cup. Add the tea and sugar finding your own
sweet balance. Mix with the stick of cinnamon.*

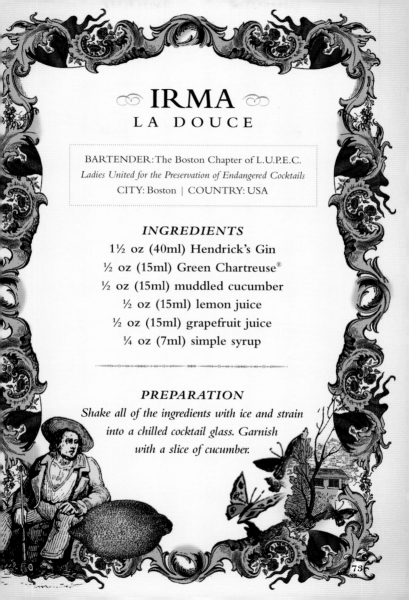

❧ IRMA ❧
LA DOUCE

BARTENDER: The Boston Chapter of L.U.P.E.C.
Ladies United for the Preservation of Endangered Cocktails
CITY: Boston | COUNTRY: USA

INGREDIENTS
1½ oz (40ml) Hendrick's Gin
½ oz (15ml) Green Chartreuse®
½ oz (15ml) muddled cucumber
½ oz (15ml) lemon juice
½ oz (15ml) grapefruit juice
¼ oz (7ml) simple syrup

PREPARATION
*Shake all of the ingredients with ice and strain
into a chilled cocktail glass. Garnish
with a slice of cucumber.*

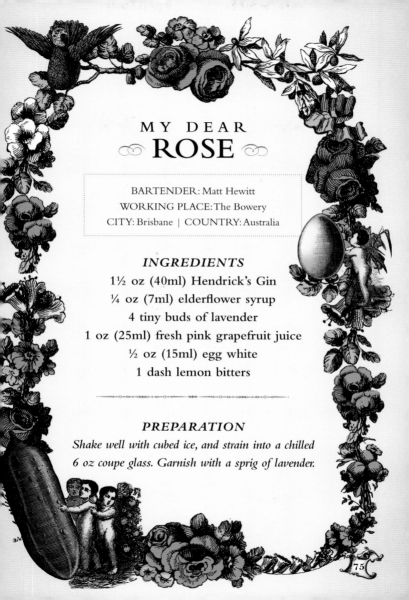

MY DEAR
∽ ROSE ∽

BARTENDER: Matt Hewitt
WORKING PLACE: The Bowery
CITY: Brisbane | COUNTRY: Australia

INGREDIENTS
1½ oz (40ml) Hendrick's Gin
¼ oz (7ml) elderflower syrup
4 tiny buds of lavender
1 oz (25ml) fresh pink grapefruit juice
½ oz (15ml) egg white
1 dash lemon bitters

PREPARATION
Shake well with cubed ice, and strain into a chilled 6 oz coupe glass. Garnish with a sprig of lavender.

LONDON
CALLING

BARTENDER: Christopher Jepson
WORKING PLACE: St. Martin's Lane
CITY: London | COUNTRY: England

INGREDIENTS

1¾ oz (50ml) Hendrick's Gin

3 dashes orange bitters

½ oz (15ml) fresh lemon juice

¼ oz (10ml) simple syrup

½ oz (15ml) Spanish dry sherry

PREPARATION

Shake all ingredients and serve in a cocktail glass.

MINT 500

BARTENDER: Jason Scott
WORKING PLACE: Bramble
CITY: Edinburgh | COUNTRY: Scotland

INGREDIENTS

1¾ oz (50ml) Hendrick's Gin

½ oz (12.5ml) lime juice

dash elderflower cordial

½ oz (12.5ml) apple juice

6 mint leaves

2 basil leaves

8 dashes peach bitters

¾ oz (20ml) vanilla gomme syrup

dash pasteurised egg white

PREPARATION

Place all of the ingredients into a shaker and 'dry' shake.
Then fill the shaker with ice and shake vigorously again.
Double strain and garnish with a cupped basil leaf.

SILVER HOUND
COBBLER

BARTENDER: Ago Perrone
WORKING PLACE: Connaught Bar at Connaught Hotel
CITY: London | COUNTRY: England

INGREDIENTS

1¼ oz (35ml) Hendrick's Gin
1 oz (25ml) ginger wine
⅛ oz (5ml) simple syrup
1 ¾ oz (50ml) silver tea

PREPARATION

*Muddle and stir all of the ingredients in a
mixing glass. Strain on a chunk of ice and garnish
with a cucumber spiral, strawberry
and grated nutmeg.*

THE USUAL
SUSPECTS

BARTENDER: Jim Meehan
WORKING PLACE: PDT
CITY: New York City | COUNTRY: USA

INGREDIENTS
2 oz (60ml) Hendrick's Gin
¾ oz (20ml) Lillet® Blanc
¾ oz (20ml) French dry vermouth
2 drops of rose flower water

PREPARATION
Add everything to a mixing glass, then add ice. Stir and strain into a chilled coupe. Rub a thin slice of English cucumber around the rim and float on the surface.

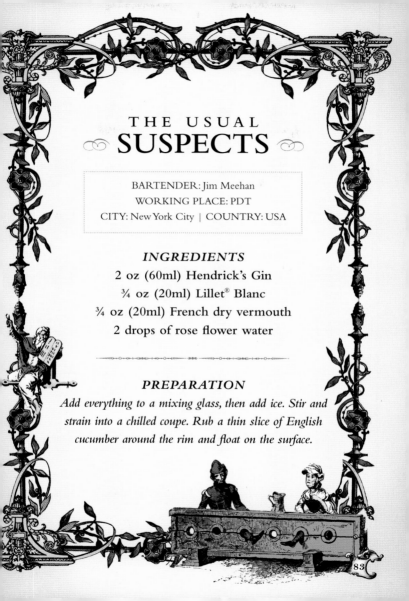

UP ROSE

BARTENDER: Hidetsugu Ueno
WORKING PLACE: High Five
CITY: Tokyo | COUNTRY: Japan

INGREDIENTS

1¾ oz (50ml) Hendrick's Gin
¼ oz (10ml) Muscat liqueur
⅛ oz (5ml) Green Chartreuse®
⅛ oz (5ml) Scotch Whisky liqueur

PREPARATION

Build ingredients in a tumbler and gently stir.

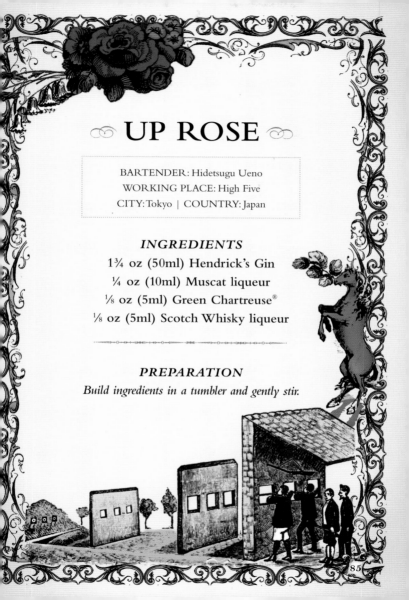

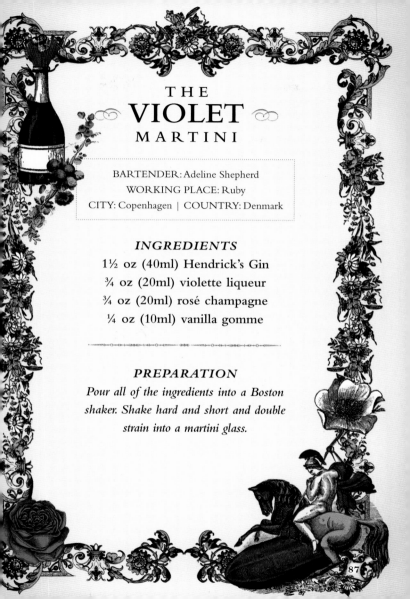

THE
VIOLET
MARTINI

BARTENDER: Adeline Shepherd
WORKING PLACE: Ruby
CITY: Copenhagen | COUNTRY: Denmark

INGREDIENTS

1½ oz (40ml) Hendrick's Gin
¾ oz (20ml) violette liqueur
¾ oz (20ml) rosé champagne
¼ oz (10ml) vanilla gomme

PREPARATION

Pour all of the ingredients into a Boston shaker. Shake hard and short and double strain into a martini glass.

HENDRICK'S
EXPERIENCE 1

BARTENDERS: Romée de Goriainoff,
Pierre Charles Cros and Olivier Bon
WORKING PLACE: Experimental Cocktail Club
CITY: Paris | COUNTRY: France

INGREDIENTS
1¾ oz (50ml) Hendrick's Gin
¾ oz (20ml) Belvoir® elderflower cordial
¾ oz (20ml) fresh lemon juice
2 basil leaves
muddled lemon grass

PREPARATION
Shake well and serve in a martini glass.

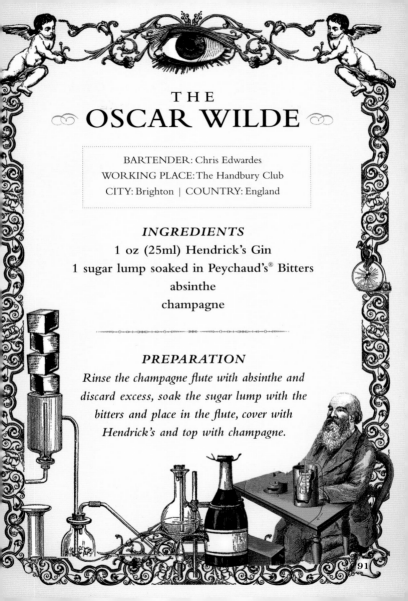

THE
OSCAR WILDE

BARTENDER: Chris Edwardes
WORKING PLACE: The Handbury Club
CITY: Brighton | COUNTRY: England

INGREDIENTS

1 oz (25ml) Hendrick's Gin
1 sugar lump soaked in Peychaud's® Bitters
absinthe
champagne

PREPARATION

*Rinse the champagne flute with absinthe and
discard excess, soak the sugar lump with the
bitters and place in the flute, cover with
Hendrick's and top with champagne.*

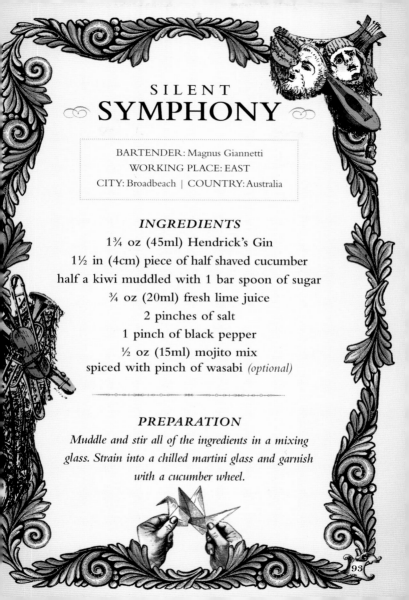

SILENT
SYMPHONY

BARTENDER: Magnus Giannetti
WORKING PLACE: EAST
CITY: Broadbeach | COUNTRY: Australia

INGREDIENTS

1¾ oz (45ml) Hendrick's Gin

1½ in (4cm) piece of half shaved cucumber

half a kiwi muddled with 1 bar spoon of sugar

¾ oz (20ml) fresh lime juice

2 pinches of salt

1 pinch of black pepper

½ oz (15ml) mojito mix
spiced with pinch of wasabi *(optional)*

PREPARATION

Muddle and stir all of the ingredients in a mixing glass. Strain into a chilled martini glass and garnish with a cucumber wheel.

ST. CLEMENTS

BARTENDER: Johan Gelderblom
WORKING PLACE: Long Bar at Sanderson
CITY: London | COUNTRY: England

INGREDIENTS

1¾ oz (50ml) Hendrick's Gin
1 oz (25ml) lemon juice
¾ oz (20ml) simple syrup
Schweppes® bitter lemon

PREPARATION

Shake well and strain into a highball glass.
Top with Schweppes® bitter lemon.
Garnish with an orange wheel.

⊱ OPIUM ⊰

BARTENDER: Miguel Setién
WORKING PLACE: Ramses
CITY: Madrid | COUNTRY: Spain

INGREDIENTS

4 oz (120ml) Hendrick´s Gin

3 or 4 pieces of green apple

1 oz (30ml) simple syrup

1 dash lime cordial

1 dash Blue Tropic®

PREPARATION

Put the apple into a shaker tin and crush it. Add the
Hendrick's Gin, simple syrup and lime cordial.
Shake all ingredients except Blue Tropic.®
Pour the Blue Tropic® into a martini
glass and lay the mix of
the shaker on top.

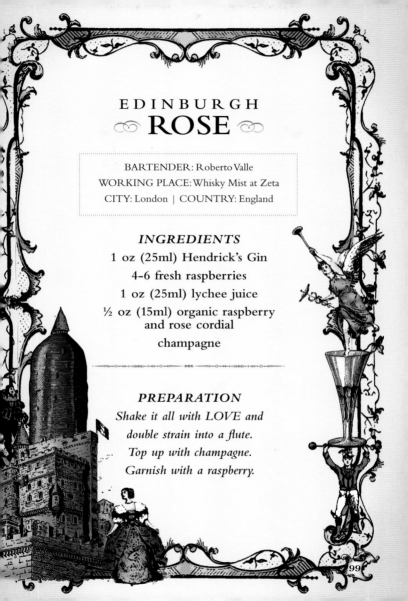

EDINBURGH
ROSE

BARTENDER: Roberto Valle
WORKING PLACE: Whisky Mist at Zeta
CITY: London | COUNTRY: England

INGREDIENTS

1 oz (25ml) Hendrick's Gin

4-6 fresh raspberries

1 oz (25ml) lychee juice

½ oz (15ml) organic raspberry
and rose cordial

champagne

PREPARATION

Shake it all with LOVE and
double strain into a flute.
Top up with champagne.
Garnish with a raspberry.

HENDRICK'S
GIN BLAZER

BARTENDER: Xavier Padovani
WORKING PLACE: Bar Mama Shelter
CITY: Paris | COUNTRY: France

INGREDIENTS
1½ oz (40ml) Hendrick's Gin
½ oz (15ml) Green Chartreuse®
fresh branch of rosemary

PREPARATION
*Infuse rosemary in Hendrick's Gin and
Green Chartreuse.® Flame Jerry Thomas style.
Serve in a teacup.*

CARTE BLANCHE

BARTENDER: Jim Ryan
Hendrick's Brand Ambassador
COUNTRY: USA

INGREDIENTS

1½ oz (40ml) Hendrick's Gin
2 wheels of English cucumber
½ oz (15ml) fresh lime juice
¼ oz (7ml) simple syrup
2 healthy dashes Regan's® orange bitters
dry sparkling wine

PREPARATION

*Pour all ingredients in a mixing glass.
Shake with vigour and double strain into a
cocktail glass. Top with bone dry sparkling
wine, and garnish with a cucumber wheel.*

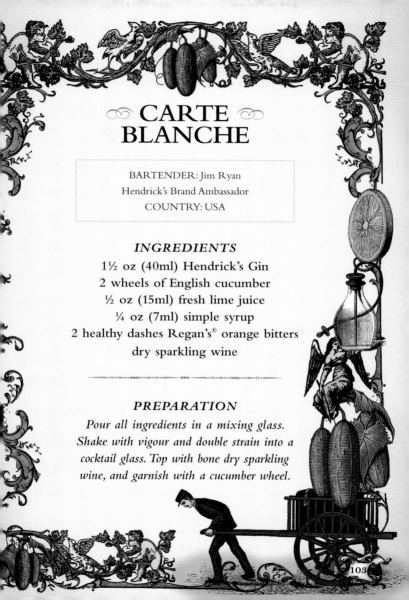

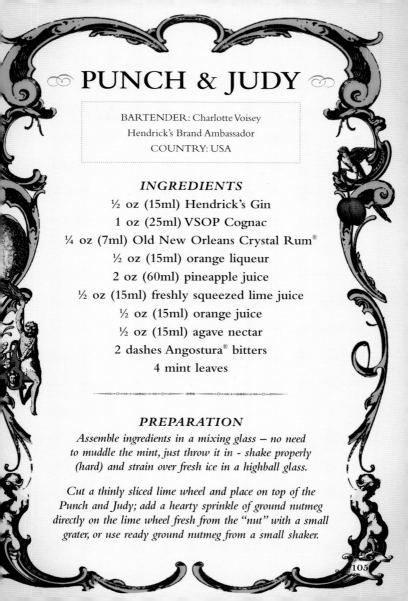

PUNCH & JUDY

BARTENDER: Charlotte Voisey
Hendrick's Brand Ambassador
COUNTRY: USA

INGREDIENTS

½ oz (15ml) Hendrick's Gin

1 oz (25ml) VSOP Cognac

¼ oz (7ml) Old New Orleans Crystal Rum®

½ oz (15ml) orange liqueur

2 oz (60ml) pineapple juice

½ oz (15ml) freshly squeezed lime juice

½ oz (15ml) orange juice

½ oz (15ml) agave nectar

2 dashes Angostura® bitters

4 mint leaves

PREPARATION

*Assemble ingredients in a mixing glass – no need
to muddle the mint, just throw it in - shake properly
(hard) and strain over fresh ice in a highball glass.*

*Cut a thinly sliced lime wheel and place on top of the
Punch and Judy; add a hearty sprinkle of ground nutmeg
directly on the lime wheel fresh from the "nut" with a small
grater, or use ready ground nutmeg from a small shaker.*

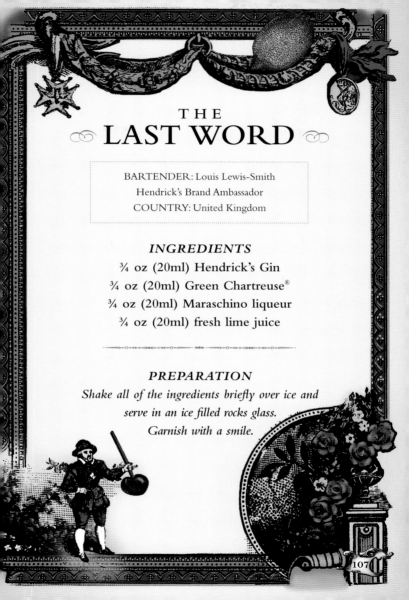

THE
~ LAST WORD ~

BARTENDER: Louis Lewis–Smith

Hendrick's Brand Ambassador

COUNTRY: United Kingdom

INGREDIENTS

¾ oz (20ml) Hendrick's Gin

¾ oz (20ml) Green Chartreuse®

¾ oz (20ml) Maraschino liqueur

¾ oz (20ml) fresh lime juice

PREPARATION

Shake all of the ingredients briefly over ice and
serve in an ice filled rocks glass.
Garnish with a smile.

UNUSUAL
BRAZILIAN
GIN

BARTENDER: Fran Olmo
Hendrick's Brand Ambassador
COUNTRY: Spain

INGREDIENTS

2 oz (60ml) Hendrick's Gin
4 pieces melon
1 oz (30ml) simple syrup
1 dash melon liqueur

PREPARATION

*Put the pieces of melon into an old fashioned glass
and crush it with the syrup. Fill to the top with frappé ice
and pour over Hendrick's Gin. At last, a dash of melon
liqueur and serve with two straws. Mix it from the bottom up.
This cocktail is made like a caipirinha: same glass and
decoration, but with melon instead of lemon and
Hendrick's Gin instead of Cachaça.*

HOT GIN
PUNCH

BARTENDER: Xavier Padovani
HENDRICK'S GLOBAL BRAND AMBASSADOR

SERVES 6

INGREDIENTS

3 teacups Hendrick's Gin

3 teacups Madeira wine

3 cloves

a pinch grated nutmeg

1 large teaspoon cinnamon powder

1 teaspoon brown sugar

6 large lemon twists

1 small slice orange

3 big chunks fresh pineapple

4 large spoons honey

lemon juice

dash water

PREPARATION

*Combine all of the ingredients in a small pot and simmer
gently for 30 minutes. Pour into a teapot and serve
hot in teacups with some gingerbread on the side.*

*This recipe has been adapted from the original 1850 recipe
found in the book "Drinking with Dickens" by Cedric Dickens,
Great-Grandson of Charles Dickens.*

HENDRICK'S
BREEZE

INGREDIENTS
1½ oz (40ml) Hendrick's Gin
2 oz (60ml) white cranberry juice
splash of Fresca

PREPARATION
Build over ice in a tall glass.
Garnish with orange and lemon wheel.

SERGEANT
SUNSPLASH

INGREDIENTS
1½ oz (40ml) Hendrick's Gin
½ oz (15ml) Licor 43®
1 oz (30ml) fresh orange juice
½ oz (15ml) fresh lemon juice
½ oz (15ml) simple syrup

PREPARATION
Assemble ingredients and shake well with
plenty of ice. Serve in a long glass and
garnish with a cucumber slice.

HENDRICK'S
MARTINI

INGREDIENTS

1½ oz (40ml) Hendrick's Gin
¾ oz (20ml) dry vermouth

PREPARATION

Stir vermouth and Hendrick's Gin
over ice cubes in a mixing glass.
Strain into a martini glass.
Garnish with a cucumber slice.

CUCUMBER
ROYALE

INGREDIENTS
1 oz (30ml) Hendrick's Gin
½ oz (15ml) cucumber vodka
½ oz (15ml) elderflower cordial
champagne

PREPARATION
*Gently stir together Hendrick's Gin,
cucumber vodka, elderflower
cordial and champagne.*

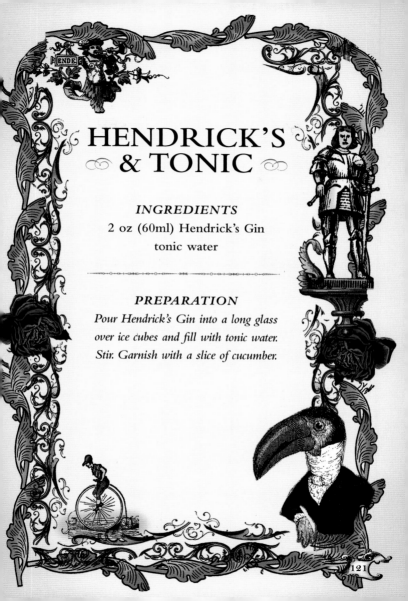

HENDRICK'S & TONIC

INGREDIENTS

2 oz (60ml) Hendrick's Gin
tonic water

PREPARATION

*Pour Hendrick's Gin into a long glass
over ice cubes and fill with tonic water.
Stir. Garnish with a slice of cucumber.*

BARWARE

AND GLASSWARE

*O*f course the quality of a cocktail has most to do with the ingredients contained therein, but a comprehensive collection of bar equipment at one's disposal can vastly improve the calibre of any cocktail.

THE BOSTON SHAKER

(and its associate, the Hawthorne Strainer)

The Boston Shaker consists of a stainless steel container, one glass, and no strainer – thereby creating the opportunity to use the marvellous Hawthorne. The Hawthorne Strainer uses a rolled spring on its edge for the thoughtful purpose of permitting fruit pulp and even some pleasant slivers of ice to enter the glass. The resulting intangible subtleties tend to create a finer cocktail, particularly when combined with the exquisite subtleties of Hendrick's.

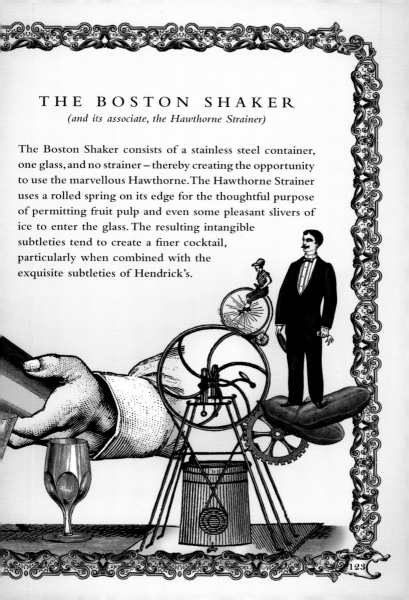

SELF-POURING
TEAPOT

One of the greatest labour-saving devices of all time, the self-pouring teapot is the perfect companion to a set of Teatime Martini Glasses, especially when filled with Hendrick's Gin. No heavy lifting is necessary: simply press the top and its libations will flow forth.

THE CUCUMBER
BALLER

A must-have for any establishment serving Hendrick's, this ingenious device was born into the world for the delightfully particular function of scooping out ball-shaped globes of cucumber *(an oddly satisfying activity, we must say)*.

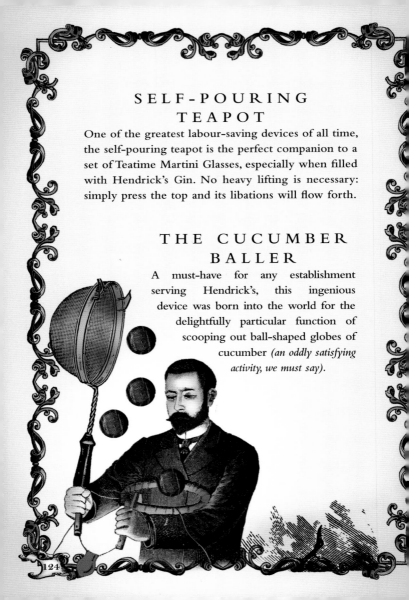

THE COLLINS GLASS

The vertically inclined cousin of the highball, the Collins is taller and slender in proportion. Its shape makes it particularly well suited to sit comfortably in the palm of the hand and often initiates small talk concerning the proficiency of opposable thumbs.

The YARD GLASS

A yard long in length, this glass begins with a wide mouth at the top and tapers over the entire length to the bottom, which is shaped into a bulb. Expressly designed for drinking ale, we've found the yard glass is better put to use as a decorative goldfish bowl behind the bar.

HENDRICK'S
DISTILLED and BOTTLED IN SCOTLAND
GIN
EST. 1886

TEATIME
MARTINI GLASS

Pause for a moment and seriously consider why one would prefer to sip tea when they could quaff a teatime martini instead. Precisely! The Teatime Martini Glass is a remarkable fusion of the martini glass and the teacup, creating a peculiarly appropriate vessel for the teatime cocktail.

CUCUMBER
PEELER

Few bar accoutrements are more impressive to a discerning tippler than the cucumber peeler. Engineered to precisely remove the fruit's outer skin, the peeler allows for an incredibly impressive array of cucumber garnish options.

THE SOUR GLASS

Looking very much like a miniature wine glass, the sour glass' express purpose in life is to hold the classic mid-nineteenth century cocktail from whence it takes its name. We would be remiss not to mention the fact that a Hendrick's Sour – of which there are several varieties – makes use of this glass quite nicely.

THE CUCUMBER POT

(a most helpful item)

The cucumber offers a rejuvenatingly fresh and subtle range of flavour sensations that are more delicate than the comparatively overpowering flavour of humdrum citrus garnishes. To keep one's cucumber maximally fresh, our distillery staff recommends this strangely beautiful Cucumber Pot.

The SWISS ARMY
BAR TOOL

From its removable swizzle stick and spirit-proof pen, to its foldout-magnifying monocle and high-pitched tippler whistle – perfect for removing rowdy patrons from the bar after last call – the Swiss army bar tool is indispensable for the master mixologist.

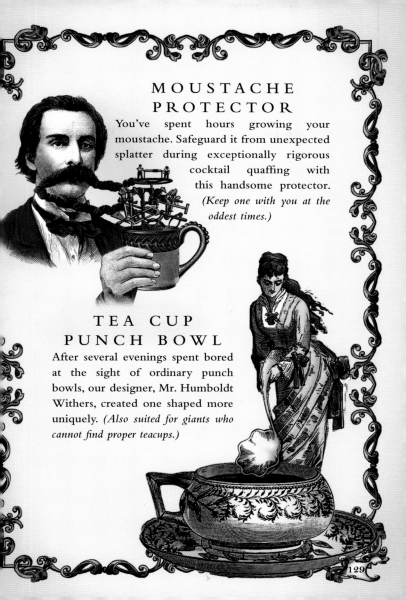

MOUSTACHE PROTECTOR

You've spent hours growing your moustache. Safeguard it from unexpected splatter during exceptionally rigorous cocktail quaffing with this handsome protector. *(Keep one with you at the oddest times.)*

TEA CUP PUNCH BOWL

After several evenings spent bored at the sight of ordinary punch bowls, our designer, Mr. Humboldt Withers, created one shaped more uniquely. *(Also suited for giants who cannot find proper teacups.)*

THE PIANOCKTAIL

*O*f all inventions that the modern musical, literary and drinking sciences have provided us, Boris Vian's Pianocktail far surpasses all others in its ingenuity. The Pianocktail is a piano whose ivory keys have been carefully calibrated to mix a different cocktail in accordance to the tune that is played. With the press of each key, a small amount of a particular spirit is released into the glasses hidden behind the piano's front panel.

Never has a cocktail harmonised so perfectly with mood; each tipple tastes as the music it was prepared to sounds. A favourite amongst Dixieland jazz enthusiasts, pianists of all genres would no more make a "Chopsticks" than a barman would mix a Hendrick's and Tonic. However, no attempts at making a 4'33" by experimental composer John Cage have yet proven successful.

UNUSUAL PLACES
TO ENJOY YOUR

HENDRICK'S®
GIN

*W*hile we do espouse the virtues of a well-equipped bar, we firmly believe that a bottle of Hendrick's can be put to good use in pretty much any location one might find oneself. For example:

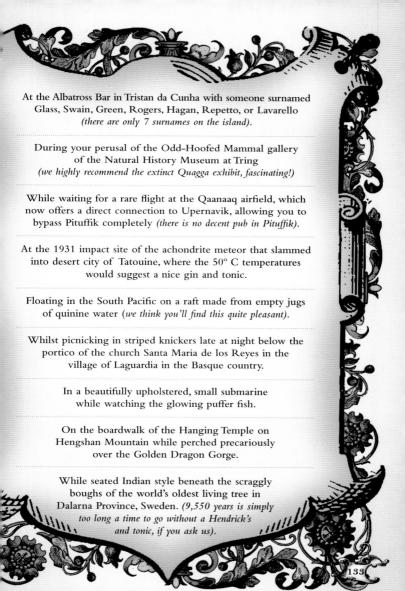

At the Albatross Bar in Tristan da Cunha with someone surnamed Glass, Swain, Green, Rogers, Hagan, Repetto, or Lavarello *(there are only 7 surnames on the island).*

During your perusal of the Odd-Hoofed Mammal gallery of the Natural History Museum at Tring *(we highly recommend the extinct Quagga exhibit, fascinating!)*

While waiting for a rare flight at the Qaanaaq airfield, which now offers a direct connection to Upernavik, allowing you to bypass Pituffik completely *(there is no decent pub in Pituffik).*

At the 1931 impact site of the achondrite meteor that slammed into desert city of Tatouine, where the 50° C temperatures would suggest a nice gin and tonic.

Floating in the South Pacific on a raft made from empty jugs of quinine water *(we think you'll find this quite pleasant).*

Whilst picnicking in striped knickers late at night below the portico of the church Santa María de los Reyes in the village of Laguardia in the Basque country.

In a beautifully upholstered, small submarine while watching the glowing puffer fish.

On the boardwalk of the Hanging Temple on Hengshan Mountain while perched precariously over the Golden Dragon Gorge.

While seated Indian style beneath the scraggly boughs of the world's oldest living tree in Dalarna Province, Sweden. *(9,550 years is simply too long a time to go without a Hendrick's and tonic, if you ask us).*

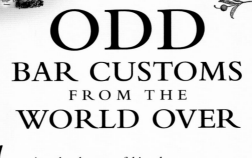

ODD
BAR CUSTOMS
FROM THE
WORLD OVER

*A*s mentioned at the start of this volume, one must venture far and wide to find the small, but ever growing, group of individuals who love Hendrick's dearly. We know this because we dispatched our staff anthropologist, Professor Eustace Hembry, years ago on an extensive expedition to find these people wherever they may be. During his travels, Eustace encountered many strange drinking rituals. We've recounted these fascinating practices in this volume in the hopes that our readers will behave appropriately in the company of any fellow Hendrick's drinkers they might encounter the world over.

A cautionary note: Professor Hembry is a well qualified anthropologist, yet somewhat of a tippler.
We prefer not to guarantee his findings.

DRINKING
from the HORN

NORWAY

In accordance with ancient Viking drinking rituals, a "drinking horn" is passed around in a circle and each recipient makes a toast, oath, or boast, before sipping from the communal cup. *(Professor Hembry improvised by reading his luggage tag.)*

The PICKLED CUCUMBER CHASER

UKRAINE

One shot of vodka is chased with another shot of vodka, pursued by the smelling and subsequent eating of a gherkin. *(For the record, we approve of neither the vodka, nor the bastardisation of the cucumber.)*

"We shall TOAST THEM ATOP their STEEDS!"

SOUTHWEST CHINA

The Naxi people prefer not to wait until guests are seated at the table to make a toast in their honour; instead, tradition dictates that hosts greet their guests outside of the home and toast them before they are able to dismount their horse.

BRUDERSCHAFT

GERMANY

If two Germans decide that their relationship has progressed beyond the point of formal address, they consummate the newly recognised informality by linking arms and quaffing their beverages.

The EYEPATCH ROUND

UPPER MONGOLIA

It is customary for the first person that spots a man wearing an eyepatch to buy a round of drinks for everyone.

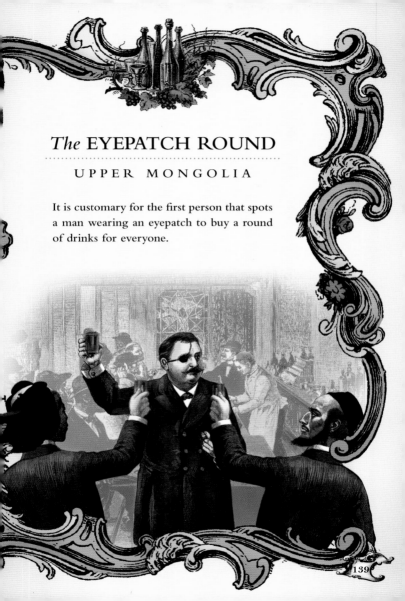

The BRIM TAP.
The COMMERCIAL, GIRVAN

SCOTLAND

When generous tipper Walter McGifney thumps the brim of his hat three times at the bar, it indicates he is ordering a double without the knowledge of the ever-present Mrs. McGifney.

The ICELANDIC OLIVE TOSS

ICELAND

In Sakhatvik, Iceland, a gentleman who wants to approach a lady will toss an olive into her drink. *(We ourselves draw the line at tossing an olive into a frozen daiquiri. Of course, the odds of our being attracted to a daiquiri drinker are long indeed.)*

USELESS USES

HENDRICK'S BOTTLE

has BEEN PUT

fig.1

A pig MILKER

*I*n our tireless efforts to protect the most unusual world in which we live, Hendrick's would like people to know that while empty bottles are inevitable, these precious vessels need not be discarded. There exist a number of unusual uses to which an empty Hendrick's bottle can be put. A few suggestions:

fig.3
A LIGHTHOUSE
for ladybirds

fig.2
An aardvark
TRAP

fig.5
A polar bear
TEETHING RING

fig.4
A BASKET *for a*
snake-charmer's snake

143

Croquet players rely heavily on Newtonian physics when making intricate calculations in regards to ball dynamics, mallet vectors and when to break for gin and tonics.

Augustus, the village rapscallion, rearranges wickets on the back nine while the crowd is preoccupied with the stroke at hand.

A platter of controversially prepared finger sandwiches incites angry titters among the crowd.

*F*ew pl
exhilarating than the cro
midsummer's match. Th
on a cool Hendr

Before Miranda Ballbasher stepped onto the lawn a few years ago at Lindensh Lawn and broke the gender barrier with a fantastic come-from-beh win in the finals, men a women had competed in separate leagues. No lon

"Will the pinky hold prevail?" Emil Laxhe renowned croquet commentator and hal of-famer, whispers int the megaphone with enough tension that in attendance take a mighty quaff of gin calm their nerves.

QUET MATCH

nore
in the midst of a
no better place to sip
Tonic.

The ever-vigilant, all-volunteer croquet-lawn security force charges the lawn upon spying Augustus' mischief making.

The woman waving he Hendrick's bottle interrupted Bertram's concentration, provoking nental fantasies of an excellent dry gin nartini.

Holding aloft a half-filled Hendrick's bottle, Elana cheers on home-town heartthrob Bertram "The Mallet" von Tilley.

"The match is not over until the cat lady sings!" yelled Milo Cavendish, earnestly searching the crowd for Mrs. Featherflot, the town spinster.

BECAUSE QUITE SIMPLY,
the HUMDRUM
is hardly NEWSWORTHY.

the Unus

A review

HENDRICK'S GIN

il Times.net

things unusual

Reach instead for the review of
ALL THINGS
UNUSUAL.

BROUGHT TO YOU *by the* PURVEYORS
of A MOST UNUSUAL GIN.